Student Performance

Music Theory in Band and Orchestra

by Wendy Barden

To my son, Kevin, an architect who continues to find joy, solace, and inspiration in music.

ISBN-10: 0-8497-2612-3
ISBN-13: 978-0-8497-2612-5

© **2009 Kjos Music Press**. 4382 Jutland Drive, San Diego, California, 92117.
International copyright secured. All rights reserved. Printed in U.S.A.
WARNING! Governments around the world provide copyright laws to encourage composition and publication of new music. Anyone copying music without permission is breaking the copyright law and is subject to penalties. Please do not violate copyright laws. Do not copy or reproduce the contents of this book except where authorized. Thank you!

W67

Table of Contents

Practical Music Theory

Students join band or orchestra to learn to play an instrument. Students expect to play that instrument well as a result of their enrollment and continued participation in the program. Their parents, the school board, and the community-at-large have the same expectation. Fairly or not, the ensemble and music program are often judged by the quality of the performances.

At all levels, much goes into learning concert repertoire. You are teaching new notes and fingerings, new rhythms, shaping phrases, improving intonation, refining articulation or bowing styles, developing technique, and balancing melody and harmony parts in every piece. How can you incorporate music theory into the rehearsal, too?

If you are thinking there is not enough time to teach music theory along with preparing four to six pieces for the next concert, consider this. The more students understand about the music, the better they will be able to perform it and the more they will enjoy it. An understanding of music theory will help improve the performance of every band and orchestra.

That may be a bold statement, but it is corroborated by several initiatives in the United States over the past four decades. The Wisconsin Comprehensive Musicianship through Performance Project began in 1977 with the primary goal of "performance with understanding." Students develop an understanding of musical elements connected to the pieces they are performing, and advance their thinking to higher levels.[1] A similar project has been developed in Iowa, where many directors continue to ask themselves, "Is my instrumental music program creating knowledgeable musicians?"[2]

The voluntary National Standards for Music Education were developed through a consortium of national arts education organizations and were adopted in 1994. The standards include a variety of music skills, concepts, and experiences that come together in a comprehensive music education that includes music theory. Content standards #5 and #6 address developing knowledge and skills in music theory. "Learning to read and notate music gives [students] a skill with which to explore music independently and with others. Listening to, analyzing, and evaluating music are important building blocks of musical learning."[3]

In the years following the adoption of the national standards, most states and local school districts developed standards in music education that include recognizing, understanding, describing, and applying the elements of music. Performance is only one facet of the learning that takes place in instrumental music ensembles.

Practically speaking, a comprehensive music education starts with the careful selection of repertoire for your band or orchestra. Rhythm is one of the key factors directors consider when selecting repertoire, especially for beginning ensembles. You can help students understand the rhythms they are performing by teaching the concepts in depth, checking for understanding in a variety of ways, and providing opportunities to apply their learning to new situations.

A second factor in the selection of repertoire is exposure to a variety of genres including theme and variations, marches, and program music. Again, you can help students develop understanding of musical elements used in these varied pieces by applying the elements in performance, and extending learning to higher levels with tasks such as these:

- *Theme and variations.* Have students describe the theme in musical terms. Compare variations to the theme and one another—how are they similar and how are they different in terms of rhythm and meter, dynamics, tempo, articulation/bowing styles, tonality? Create new variations.
- *Marches.* Have students compare dynamics or articulation/bowing styles. Change the dynamics or style—how does that change the sound of the piece? Consider how the composer might feel about the changes. Evaluate the ensemble's performance to an exemplary model.
- *Program music.* Choose an image and have students describe what the music might sound like if it were to convey the same mood or feeling—rhythm and meter, dynamics, tempo, articulation/bowing styles, tonality?

The more students know about the music, the better they will be able to perform it.

It can be tricky to incorporate music theory activities when the ensemble is large or there is minimal rehearsal time, but it's not impossible.

- *Is there more to teaching terms and symbols than memorizing definitions?* Yes! Bloom's Taxonomy of higher-level thinking adapted to music learning begins on page 5. ➳
- *What strategies can be used to teach music theory?* A discussion of instructional strategies begins on page 9. ➳
- *How can you develop appropriate activities and assessments?* A variety of forms begins on page 12. ➳

The intention of this book is to share research-based strategies for maximizing student performance in band or orchestra through practical attention to music theory. Critical to these strategies is teaching music theory through repertoire, and connecting and expanding experiences to promote higher-level thinking.

Instead of thinking "yes, but..." consider "yes, and... ." When music theory concepts are learned and understood, the ensemble's next performance will be at the highest possible level!

Hierarchy of Thinking Skills

The first steps to learning music theory involve memorization—facts, definitions, patterns, and concepts. Once students are able to define terms and symbols or count rhythms, they can apply that knowledge to their concert music, but don't stop there. Learning becomes increasingly sophisticated when students also use the concepts in analyzing music, evaluating their performance against an exemplary model, and composing or improvising new melodies. The hierarchy of cognitive skills just described—from memorization to creation—is shown below.

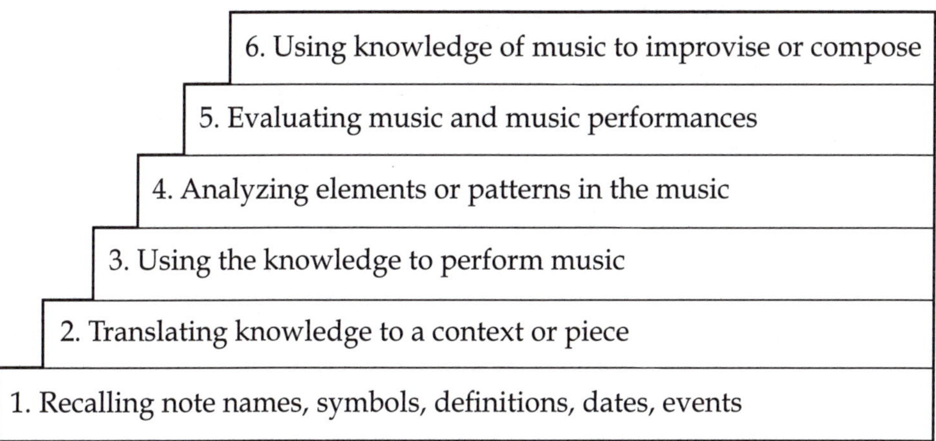
6. Using knowledge of music to improvise or compose
5. Evaluating music and music performances
4. Analyzing elements or patterns in the music
3. Using the knowledge to perform music
2. Translating knowledge to a context or piece
1. Recalling note names, symbols, definitions, dates, events

This hierarchy is based on Bloom's Taxonomy (1956) which was one of the first systems to order thinking and learning. The taxonomy was developed by Benjamin Bloom and a team of educational psychologists for the purpose of classifying educational objectives. It has since been applied across many fields including education, business, and medicine. For our purposes, the taxonomy delineates a pathway for moving the short-term memorization of music theory concepts to a deeper, more meaningful level of learning.

In 2001, five decades after the original taxonomy was published, Lorin Anderson led the development of the Revised Bloom's Taxonomy. He and his team revised the terminology of the taxonomy, reordered the highest levels (to the order shown in the chart above) because they believed creative thinking is more complex than critical thinking, and expanded Bloom's original work to show the intersection of knowledge and procedure. The more detailed hierarchy on the next page suggests specific applications to musical learning.[4]

Revised Bloom's Taxonomy (2001) and Music Learning

Cognitive Skills	Music-Specific Objectives
6. Creating Arranging Composing Designing Improvising	◆ Compose a new accompaniment for a folk song. ◆ Arrange a hymn for brass quartet. ◆ Improvise background music for a class video project.
5. Evaluating Criticizing Judging Justifying Recommending	◆ Evaluate the accuracy of the ensemble's performance. ◆ Justify the choice of music for a specific performance. ◆ Recommend an outstanding performance or recording of Debussy's *La Mer*.
4. Analyzing Comparing Contrasting Differentiating Discriminating	◆ Describe how the phrases are similar and/or different. ◆ Contrast the theme and two variations. ◆ Compare the harmonic progression of two Beatles' songs.
3. Applying Demonstrating Manipulating Performing Producing	◆ Demonstrate loud and soft notes on an instrument. ◆ Play a legato melody on your instrument with characteristic tone. ◆ Play the B♭ Concert chromatic scale with alternate fingerings.
2. Understanding Classifying Converting Extending Rewriting	◆ Write in the counting for a rhythm. ◆ Determine the notes in the C♯ minor scale given the formula of whole steps and half steps. ◆ Rewrite a rhythm line by replacing one note in each measure with a rest.
1. Remembering Defining Labeling Matching Naming	◆ Name the note on a particular line or space. ◆ Define a musical term or symbol. ◆ Name three significant events in Beethoven's musical career.

If you've already chosen repertoire for your next concert, how might you use the framework of Revised Bloom's Taxonomy to incorporate practical elements of music theory into your rehearsals?

Initially, attend to music theory concepts in two areas—music vocabulary and rhythm:

1. Understand that students need first to recognize terms and symbols before they will be able to perform them in concert repertoire.
2. Make teaching music vocabulary and rhythm an integral part of rehearsals. Turn to pages 49-54 for forms that may be used by stu dents to collect and define terms and symbols in their music.
3. Provide a variety of learning experiences and activities so students may practice, use, and manipulate the concepts. A discussion of ins tructional strategies begins on page 9.
4. Adapt the order of activities to progress from the bottom to the top of Revised Bloom's Taxonomy so that the activities lead student lear ning through higher and more complex levels of thinking.
5. Develop assessment tasks guided by Revised Bloom's Taxonomy to move beyond definitions. See pages 12-48 for a variety of forms.

Ultimately, extending cognitive skills to higher levels of thinking supports the high quality performances students and audience members have come to expect from your band or orchestra. The more your students understand the music theory within the concert repertoire, the better they will be able to perform it!

Activity and Assessment Design

Pre-Assessment. Chances are that years ago your band or orchestra students were introduced in general classroom music to at least some of the music theory concepts found in your current repertoire. Make no assumptions, however, about their ability to transfer their learning to the instrumental ensemble environment. Many a director has been frustrated trying to expand learning from what he or she thinks (or knows) was taught in earlier grades, only to find their students are unsuccessful.

Before you start teaching music theory, assess what students already know. They must be able to recognize terms or symbols and know their definitions before they will be able to successfully apply them in more complex experiences such as performance.

Your pre-assessment can be a short paper-and-pencil test with matching or multiple choice questions. For specific information on creating matching or multiple choice questions, turn to page 10. Matching or multiple choice questions are efficient and most useful in pre-assessment for four reasons:

- Matching and multiple choice questions can assess knowledge at the lowest levels of understanding.
- The test can be completed in a short amount of rehearsal time.
- Responses take minimal time to correct.
- You will want and need information on what each student knows.

The pre-assessment should be considered formative assessment—an activity that informs your future teaching and not one that results in a grade in the grade book.

This simple assessment will help you determine the next steps in your teaching:

- *Overall low scores?* Introduce or re-teach the concept to the full ensemble.
- *Majority of students score well?* Provide instruction or review to the small group of students who answered questions incorrectly. This could take the form of an independent study packet with feedback, working with a peer tutor, or an after-school session with you.
- *All students score well?* Move on to higher-level applications of the concept, many examples of which are shown on subsequent pages.

When all students demonstrate a basic understanding of the theory concept, the foundation is set to apply it to their performance and increasingly complex experiences following the levels of the Revised Bloom's Taxonomy. One way to maximize student performance is to engage their thinking at those higher cognitive levels.

Instructional strategies. In beginning-intermediate band and orchestra, teach music theory concepts on a need-to-know basis—when they are connected to the music you are rehearsing. It gives purpose to knowing and easily trumps the question some students are inclined to ask, "Why do we need to know this?" The ensemble's performance will be markedly better if students recognize and understand the symbols and patterns used by the composer.

Initially, attend to music theory concepts in two areas:

- Music vocabulary - dynamics, tempo, and articulation/bowing markings
- Rhythm

Music vocabulary can be learned more quickly if it is associated with a visual image. This can be especially helpful for beginning band and orchestra students for whom many terms and symbols are new. Create a glossary that has space to write the term and symbol, its definition, and an illustration. For a duplicable form template, go to page 52. For a customizable electronic version, go to the Kjos Multimedia Library at www.kjos.com.

First, use direct instruction to teach concepts and then apply the concepts to repertoire. Set up word lists or study guides. Create your own or use one of the duplicable templates on pages 49-54. At another time, have students write each word five times as they may have done for spelling words in English/Language Arts class. Practice saying terms aloud—a critical step often overlooked. Have students quiz their stand partner on music vocabulary when there are a few free minutes during the class period.

Rhythms and rhythm patterns can be learned more quickly if students are introduced to the sound before the notation. Help students experience a new rhythm from the repertoire by echoing unison patterns you play in call-and-response style. Apply the rhythm to scales and then introduce the notation symbols and write in the counting. Count, clap, and play the rhythm in exercises. Have students rewrite the exercise by substituting rests for notes. They might also complete unfinished measures or compose their own rhythm lines.

Concepts must be encountered multiple times before they are learned. Once students have memorized definitions and understand rhythms, create increasingly complex tasks so they may use the terms or rhythms in new contexts. These higher-level tasks will correlate to levels of Revised Bloom's Taxonomy and could include explaining how to perform, performing, comparing and contrasting, ordering, categorizing, interpreting, creating, composing, or arranging.

Activity and assessment tools. Paper-and-pencil activities and assessments are an integral part of the instructional process. Through these experiences you are able to engage students, expand their understanding, and monitor learning.

Activities or questions must be thoughtfully developed to balance rigor, higher-level thinking, and time. In all activities, correct answers should be clear and incorrect choices should be plausible but clearly false. Declare ahead of time how spelling, grammar, or partial answers will be scored. Humorous foils and other hints should be avoided because they will leave some students at a disadvantage.

Consider each of the following formats to best match the type and level of learning you are targeting. Generally speaking, true or false, multiple choice, and matching focus on lower-level understanding—*Remembering* and *Understanding*. Constructed response promotes higher-level thinking—*Analyzing, Evaluating,* and *Creating*.

True or false. This type of question is not used very often because students have a fifty/fifty chance of guessing the correct answer. It's possible to decrease guessing by having students rewrite a False statement into a True statement.

As an aside, questions with an "either-or" answer might be better asked orally in rehearsal. Have all students signal their respond—such as thumbs up or thumbs down—to quickly gauge basic understanding.

Multiple choice. Provide a minimum of three possible responses for each multiple choice question. Choices must be plausible to give real options. Avoid "All of the above" or "None of the above" answers especially if they are used with the intention of tricking students in minute details. There are more effective ways to tap into higher-level thinking. Multiple choice responses can be scored quickly.

Matching. Create sets of questions that are homogeneous. Limit the number of questions in each set to five so less confident readers are not overwhelmed. You want to be sure you are checking students' knowledge rather than their ability to consider a page full of choices for each question. Provide more answer choices than questions so the last item cannot be answered by default. Matching answers can be scored quickly.

Rather than a traditional format of matching choices A through F to five terms or statements, consider providing a word bank of choices. Students choose a word from a group of six and write it next to the definition, rather than writing a letter.

Constructed response. Any questions for which students provide (rather than select) the answer require deeper understanding and more time to score. If you are using constructed response activities be sure to develop sample answers and determine scoring parameters in advance.

Short-answer items require students to fill in the blank with a variety of responses including words, counting, and note names. These can provide situations that more closely match what students see in their music and experience in rehearsal, but will also take more time to score than other types of questions.

There may be times when you plan for students to write an extended response. "Writing helps students think about the content, reflect on their knowledge of the content, and share their thoughts with the teacher."[5] Writing in all content areas, including music, contributes to students' overall academic success. Be sure to give parameters about the length of response you are expecting—perhaps three sentences for younger students up to a few paragraphs for older students.

Finally, the layout of an activity, worksheet, or test requires thought because it can also support or sabotage student success. These simple guidelines can help all students better focus on the questions without becoming overwhelmed:

- Create word-processed rather than handwritten pages so letters and symbols are easy to read.
- Leave plenty of white space on the page. Instead of squeezing all of the questions onto a single page, consider spacing them out over two sides of the paper.
- Limit the number of skills or concepts addressed in each activity or assessment.
- Group types of questions and order them from simple to complex. Students will be more successful if they begin with matching or multiple choice and progress to constructed response.
- Younger students in particular will do better if they are provided with lines on which to write an answer rather than a big open space.
- Provide lines of adequate length or an adequate number of lines for their answers. For a written response with multiple lines, double space the lines.

Music theory and associated cognitive activities and assessments play an important role in the development of our students' musical learning. These experiences pull students into higher and more complex thinking, and provide a strong foundation for performance. An understanding of music theory—what's printed in the music—will help maximize student performance in your band or orchestra.

Music Vocabulary Activities and Assessments

Forms 1.1, 1.2, 1.3, 1.4, 1.5, 1.6, 1.7, 1.8, 1.9

Understanding and observing dynamic, tempo, and articulation/bowing markings can make the difference between an ordinary performance and an exciting one! Sample activities and assessment forms in this section help both directors and students think about music vocabulary as more than just definitions to memorize. Duplicate the forms or use the ideas to spark the development of your own forms specific to the music your band or orchestra is rehearsing.

Form 1.1: Matching

Goal	**Practice or assess knowledge of music vocabulary—*Remembering***
Considerations for Effective Use	◆ Use for beginning-advanced students. ◆ Create sets of items that are homogeneous so the foils are plausible. ◆ Limit the number of items in each set to five so less confident readers are not overwhelmed. ◆ Provide one or two more answer choices than the number of questions so the last item cannot be answered by default. ◆ Check your work by answering the questions, then change the order of the answers as needed to dissolve any obvious patterns. ◆ State in the instructions if answers may be used more than once. ◆ Plan on easily scoring student responses.

The form on page 13 is authorized for duplication.

For a customizable electronic version, go to the Kjos Multimedia Library at www.kjos.com.

Name ____

Match the correct definition to each term. Each letter may be used once, more than once, or not at all.

1. ______ ***forte***	A. medium loud
2. ______ ***mezzo forte***	B. soft
3. ______ ***mezzo piano***	C. medium soft
4. ______ ***piano***	D. very loud
	E. loud

---

5. ______ ***crescendo***	A. gradually softer
6. ______ ***decrescendo***	B. gradually slower
7. ______ >	C. gradually faster
8. ______ <	D. gradually louder

---

9. ______ ***ritardando***	A. return to the previous tempo
10. ______ **Allegro**	B. quick and lively
11. ______ **Moderato**	C. gradually slower
12. ______ **A tempo**	D. gradually faster
	E. medium tempo

Form 1.1: Matching

© **2009 Kjos Music Press**. This page authorized for duplication.

Form 1.2: Multiple Choice

Goal	**Practice or assess knowledge of music vocabulary—*Remembering***
Considerations for Effective Use	◆ Use for beginning-advanced students. ◆ Limit the number of possible responses per item to three or four. ◆ Write plausible foils. Avoid silly or humorous foils that may leave some students at a disadvantage. ◆ Avoid using "All of the Above" or "None of the Above" answers as a way of tricking students in minute details. ◆ Arrange choices in a logical order. ◆ Check your work by answering the questions, then change the order of the answers as needed to dissolve any obvious patterns. ◆ Plan on easily scoring student responses.

The form on page 15 is authorized for duplication.

For a customizable electronic version, go to the Kjos Multimedia Library at www.kjos.com.

Name ____

Choose the correct definition for each term and write the letter in the blank.

1. ______ ***forte***

A. medium loud
B. loud
C. very loud

2. ______ ***mezzo forte***

A. medium loud
B. loud
C. very loud

3. ______ ***mezzo piano***

A. soft
B. medium soft
C. medium loud

4. ______ ***pianissimo***

A. very soft
B. soft
C. medium soft

5. ______ ***decrescendo***

A. suddenly louder
B. gradually louder
C. gradually softer

Form 1.2: Multiple Choice

© **2009 Kjos Music Press**. This page authorized for duplication.

Form 1.3: Naming

Goal	**Practice or assess knowledge of music vocabulary—*Remembering***
Considerations for Effective Use	◆ Use for intermediate-advanced students. ◆ Increase the challenge in lower-level questions by having students provide their own answers. ◆ Plan that students will require more time to complete these questions than multiple choice or matching items. ◆ Allow more time to score student responses than for multiple choice or matching items.

The form on page 17 is authorized for duplication.

For a customizable electronic version, go to the Kjos Multimedia Library at www.kjos.com.

Name ____

Write the musical term for each symbol in the blank. Spelling must be correct to earn full credit.

1. ***mp*** ____________________

2. ***ff*** ____________________

3. ***f*** ____________________

4. ***p*** ____________________

5. ____________________

6. ____________________

7. ____________________

8. ____________________

9. ____________________

10. ____________________

Form 1.3: Naming

© **2009 Kjos Music Press**. This page authorized for duplication.

Form 1.4: True or Corrected False

Goal	**Practice or assess knowledge of music vocabulary – *Understanding***
Considerations for Effective Use	◆ Use for intermediate-advanced students. ◆ Increase the challenge in lower-level questions by having students provide their own answers. ◆ Check the order of True and False answers and as needed dissolve any obvious patterns. ◆ Provide students with an example of how to rewrite a False statement as a True one without simply inserting the word "not." ◆ This form can be used to practice or assess a variety of musical terms, such as dynamics, articulation, or styles. ◆ Plan that students will require more time to respond to these questions than multiple choice or matching items. ◆ Allow more time to score student responses due to the possible variations in changing a False statement to a True one.

The form on page 19 is authorized for duplication.

For a customizable electronic version, go to the Kjos Multimedia Library at www.kjos.com.

Name ____

If the statement is true, write **T** in the blank. If the statement is false, write **F** in the blank and rewrite the statement on the line below to make it true. Rewrite the statement without using the word "not" to earn full credit.

1.______ **Allegro** is faster than **Andante**.

____

2.______ **Andante** is faster than **Moderato**.

____

3.______ **Adagio** is faster than **Andante**.

____

4.______ ***Accelerando*** means gradually faster.

____

5.______ ***Rallentando*** and ***ritardando*** have similar meanings.

____

Form 1.4: True or Corrected False

© **2009 Kjos Music Press**. This page authorized for duplication.

Form 1.5: Categorizing

Goal	Practice or assess knowledge of music vocabulary – *Understanding*
Considerations for Effective Use	◆ Use for intermediate-advanced students. ◆ Begin all terms with either lowercase or uppercase letters. ◆ Plan on easily scoring student responses.

The form on page 21 is authorized for duplication.

For a customizable electronic version, go to the Kjos Multimedia Library at www.kjos.com.

Name ____

Assign each musical term to the correct category by writing **D** next to each dynamic marking, **T** next to each tempo marking, and **A** next to each articulation.

_______ andante	_______ staccato
_______ diminuendo	_______ fortissimo
_______ mezzo forte	_______ ritardando
_______ moderato	_______ accent
_______ allegro	_______ crescendo
_______ marcato	_______ piano

Form 1.5: Categorizing

© **2009 Kjos Music Press.** This page authorized for duplication.

Form 1.6: Ordering

Goal	**Practice or assess knowledge of music vocabulary – *Understanding***
Considerations for Effective Use	◆ Use for intermediate-advanced students. ◆ Call attention to the specified order of terms before students begin working. ◆ Two variations in format are shown. Provide a word bank of choices to make the task easier or allow students to complete the task with their own choice of terms. ◆ Plan on easily scoring student responses.

The form on page 23 is authorized for duplication.

For a customizable electronic version, go to the Kjos Multimedia Library at www.kjos.com.

Name ____

Write these tempo markings in order from slowest to fastest.

Lento	**Moderato**	**Allegro**
Vivace	**Andante**	

Slowest ______________________

____

____

____

Fastest ______________________

Write any five dynamic markings in order from softest to loudest.

Softest ______________________

____

____

____

Loudest ______________________

Form 1.6: Ordering

© **2009 Kjos Music Press.** This page authorized for duplication.

Form 1.7: Describing

Goal	**Practice or assess knowledge of music vocabulary—*Applying***
Considerations for Effective Use	◆ Use for intermediate-advanced students. ◆ Develop a list of acceptable answers before you begin scoring responses. ◆ Allow more time to score student responses due to variation in their descriptions.

The form on page 25 is authorized for duplication.

For a customizable electronic version, go to the Kjos Multimedia Library at www.kjos.com.

Name ________________________________

f *p* *f*

Look at the music example. Describe what you would need to do to play the dynamic level shown in each measure on your instrument.

Measure 1: ________________________________

Measure 2: ________________________________

Measure 3: ________________________________

Measure 4: ________________________________

Form 1.7: Describing

© **2009 Kjos Music Press.** This page authorized for duplication.

Form 1.8: Evaluating

Goal	**Practice or assess knowledge of music vocabulary—*Evaluating***
Considerations for Effective Use	◆ Use for intermediate-advanced students. ◆ Introduce this format as a discussion activity—working in small groups or partners—prior to assessment. ◆ Teach students to evaluate a recorded performance through multiple listening times. ◆ Focus students' attention on a single musical element in each listening. ◆ Plan ample time to score the variety of responses students will write.

The form on page 27 is authorized for duplication.

For a customizable electronic version, go to the Kjos Multimedia Library at www.kjos.com.

Name ________________________________ Date ______________

Title____

As we listen to the recording of this piece from yesterday's rehearsal, follow along in your music and evaluate the performance.

1. During the first playback, listen for contrast in the dynamics throughout the piece. Write at least two sentences to:

   - Describe the dynamics compared to the markings in your music.
   - Make a suggestion on how to improve our performance of dynamics.

   ____

   ____

   ____

   ____

   ____

2. During the second playback, listen for the tempo changes throughout the piece. Write at least two sentences to:

   - Describe the ensemble's execution of the tempo changes.
   - Make a suggestion on how to improve our performance.

   ____

   ____

   ____

   ____

   ____

3. During the third playback, write one sentence to compliment another instrument section on their articulation. Be specific.

   ____

   ____

Form 1.8: Evaluating

© 2009 Kjos Music Press. This page authorized for duplication.

Form 1.9: Making Compositional Decisions

Goal	**Practice or assess knowledge of music vocabulary – *Synthesizing***
Considerations for Effective Use	◆ Use for intermediate-advanced students. ◆ Introduce this format as an instructional activity – working individually or with a partner – prior to assessment. Do not use this format as part of a grade without prior experience. ◆ Limit compositional decisions to one element such as dynamics or articulation before elements are combined. ◆ Allow ample time to score the variety of responses students will write.

The form on page 29 is authorized for duplication.

For a customizable electronic version, go to the Kjos Multimedia Library at www.kjos.com.

Name ____ Date __________

Imagine you are creating a composition that suggests an occurrence in the weather. Give your new piece a title that tells something about the mood or feeling you are trying to create.

Title____

Then, describe the dynamics in your piece at the beginning, middle, and end:

- What dynamic markings have you chosen for each section?
- Why are those dynamics appropriate—what mood or feeling you are trying to communicate?

Beginning: ____

____

____

____

____

Middle: ____

____

____

____

____

End: ____

____

____

____

____

Form 1.9: Making Compositional Decisions

© **2009 Kjos Music Press.** This page authorized for duplication.

Rhythm Activities and Assessments

Forms 2.1, 2.2, 2.3, 2.4, 2.5, 2.6

Sample activities/assessment forms in this section help both directors and students think more broadly about rhythm, and apply specific rhythms to new and more complex situations. Duplicate the forms (pp. 42-48) or use the ideas to spark the development of your own forms specific to the music your band or orchestra is rehearsing.

Form 2.1: Writing the Counting

Goal	**Practice or assess knowledge of rhythm – *Understanding* and *Applying* (optional)**
Considerations for Effective Use	◆ Use for beginning-intermediate students. ◆ Create one or more counting lines from rhythms in the concert repertoire. End each line with a sense of finality. ◆ Use single-line staves. ◆ Have students either write the counting or write the counting and draw the bar lines. ◆ If notation software is used to create the counting lines, check that the spacing of the notes and rests does not give away the location of the bar lines. ◆ Plan on easily scoring student responses. ◆ Optional: Have students perform the counting line by clapping, playing on one note, or improvising a melody using one to three notes. Score the performance based on accuracy – whether the line is clapped or played on an instrument should have no bearing on the score.

For a duplicable template of Form 2.1, go to page 43.

For a customizable electronic version, go to the Kjos Multimedia Library at www.kjos.com.

Name *Alice Zabet*

Write the counting below each line.

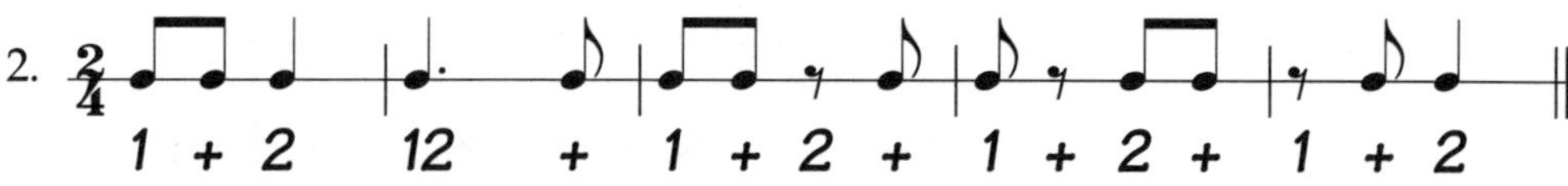

Write the counting below each line and draw the bar lines.

1\. 1 + 2 + 34 + 12 + 3 + 4 1 + 2 34

2\. 12 + 3 + 12 + 3 + 1 2 3 + 1 + 2 + 3

Sample Form 2.1: Writing the Counting

Form 2.2: Substituting Rests

Goal	Practice or assess knowledge of rhythm – *Understanding* and *Applying* (optional)
Considerations for Effective Use	◆ Use for intermediate students. ◆ Create the lines using rhythms in the concert repertoire. End each line with a sense of finality. ◆ Have students rewrite the line by substituting one note in each measure with a rest, or write the counting and then rewrite the line. ◆ Use single-line staves for both the example and response. Align the "response" staff directly under the example. ◆ Allow ample time to score the variety of responses students will write. ◆ Optional: Have students perform the counting line by clapping, playing on one note, or improvising a melody using one to three notes. Score the performance based on accuracy – whether the line is clapped or played on an instrument should have no bearing on the score.

For a duplicable template of Form 2.2, go to page 44.

For a customizable electronic version, go to the Kjos Multimedia Library at www.kjos.com.

Name *Ricky James*

Rewrite each rhythm line by replacing one note in each measure with a rest. Then, practice your new lines so you can perform them either by clapping, playing on one note, or improvising a melody using one to three notes.

Sample Form 2.2: Substituting Rests

Form 2.3: Finishing the Measures

Goal	**Practice or assess knowledge of rhythm—*Applying***
Considerations for Effective Use	◆ Use for intermediate students. ◆ Create the lines and required note values from rhythms in the concert repertoire. ◆ Always leave space for students to add the notes or rests at the end of the measure. ◆ Use single-line staves. ◆ Allow ample time to score the variety of responses students will write. ◆ Have students perform their finished lines by clapping, playing on one note, or improvising a melody using one to three notes. Score the performance based on accuracy—whether the line is clapped or played on an instrument should have no bearing on the score.

For a duplicable template of Form 2.3, go to page 45.

For a customizable electronic version, go to the Kjos Multimedia Library at www.kjos.com.

Name *Owen Thomas*

Use ♫ ♬ ♩ 𝄽 to complete the unfinished measures. End each line with a sense of finality. Then, practice your new lines so you can perform them either by clapping, playing on one note, or improvising a melody using one to three notes.

1. 

2. 

3. 

4. 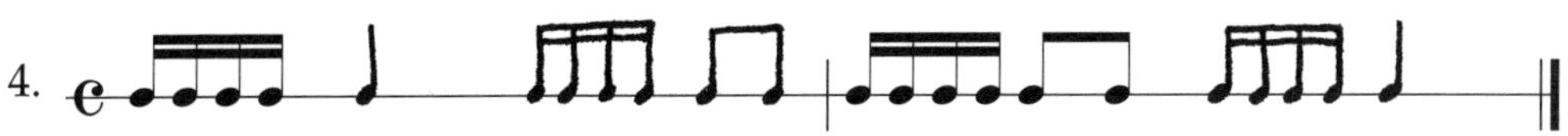

Sample Form 2.3: Finishing the Measures

Form 2.4: Performing Rhythms

Goal	Practice or assess knowledge of rhythm – *Applying*
Considerations for Effective Use	◆ Use for beginning-advanced students. ◆ Create three counting lines by re-ordering four measures from the concert repertoire. End each line with a sense of finality. ◆ Use single-line staves. ◆ Have students write the counting and practice performing each line by clapping, playing on one note, and/or improvising a melody using one to three notes. ◆ A few days later students should be prepared to perform all three lines. Select one of the three lines for each student just before they start. ◆ Score the performance based on accuracy – whether the line is clapped or played on an instrument should have no bearing on the score.

For a duplicable template of Form 2.4, go to page 46.

For a customizable electronic version, go to the Kjos Multimedia Library at www.kjos.com.

Name *Renée Morgan*

Three Rhythm Lines from Four Different Measures

- Write the counting for each line.
- Practice all lines by clapping, playing on one note, and/or improvising a melody using one to three notes.
- Your understanding of the rhythms will be assessed on *October 27*. The director will select one of the three lines and you will have the choice to clap it or play it on your instrument. Your score is based on accuracy and not by whether you clap or play.

1.
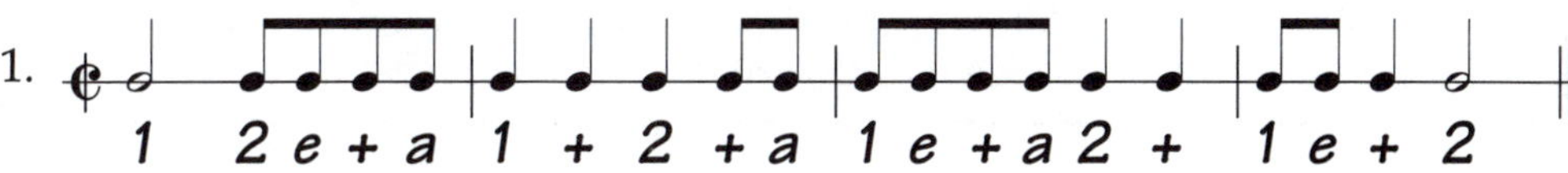

2.
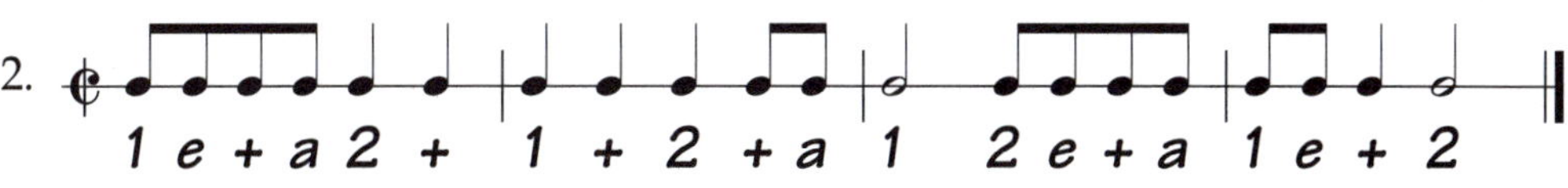

3.
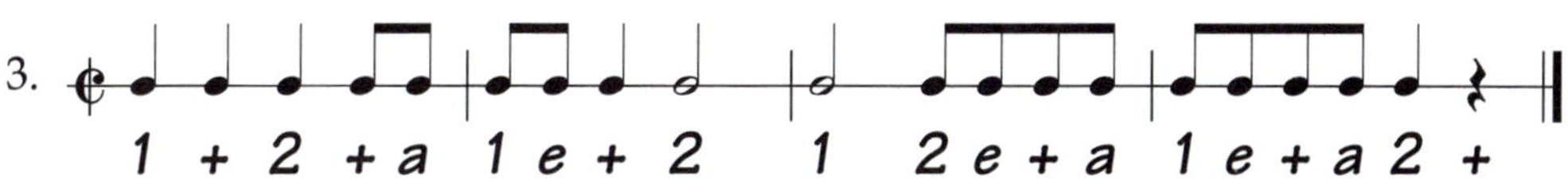

Sample Form 2.4: Performing Rhythms

Form 2.5: Evaluating a Rhythm Line

Goal	Practice or assess knowledge of rhythm – *Analyzing* and *Evaluating*
Considerations for Effective Use	◆ Use for intermediate-advanced students. ◆ Create the rhythm line and options using rhythms in the concert repertoire. ◆ Write plausible options. ◆ Use single-line staves. ◆ There is not just one correct choice to complete the rhythm line. Focus only on the reasons given for the choice and the response by the partner reviewer. ◆ Allow ample time to score the variety of responses students will write.

For a duplicable template of Form 2.5, go to page 47.

For a customizable electronic version, go to the Kjos Multimedia Library at www.kjos.com.

Name Kevin Andre

1. Your task is to assemble a rhythm line that is interesting—with both repetition and contrast—and has a sense of finality. Here is the first half of the line:

Circle the option below you think best completes the line.

2. Give two reasons why you think your choice is the best one to complete the line.

   1) Option C is the best ending because the rests make it different from the beginning.

   2) The last measure of option C sounds like it comes to rest, like it is the end.

3. Trade papers. Name of Reviewer Eddie Scott

Do you agree that the chosen option is the best one to complete the line? Why or why not?

I don't agree that option C is the best because it is too different from the first half. There should be some sixteenth notes in the last part, too.

Sample Form 2.5: Evaluating a Rhythm Line

Form 2.6: Composing a Variation

Goal	Practice or assess knowledge of rhythm – *Creating* and *Applying* (optional)
Considerations for Effective Use	◆ Use for intermediate-advanced students. ◆ Write a familiar melody such as "Twinkle, Twinkle, Little Star" as the theme. ◆ Create multiple forms of this task to provide instrument-specific clefs or transpositions of the theme. ◆ Allow ample time to score students' variations. ◆ Optional: Have students perform their theme and variation. Discuss similarities and differences among the variations.

For a duplicable template of Form 2.6, go to page 48.

For a customizable electronic version, go to the Kjos Multimedia Library at www.kjos.com.

Name *Jill King*

Create a variation of the theme.

- Use the same pitches, but change the rhythm of at least one beat in each measure to [rhythm notation]
- Determine the tempo of your variation.
- Write in dynamics and any other expressive markings and articulations/ bowings to add interest.
- Practice the theme and your variation so you can perform both.

Theme:

Variation:

Form 2.6: Composing a Variation

Duplicable Rhythm Forms

The forms on pages 43–48 are templates of the sample forms discussed in detail on pages 30–41, and are authorized for duplication. The templates are provided to help you easily adapt the activity and assessment forms to your specific classroom. The Musical Terms and Symbols reference forms on pages 50–54 are also authorized for duplication.

To prepare a form:

1. Photocopy the form.
2. Create your own lines using rhythms in the concert repertoire and write them on the form.
3. To conserve the use of paper you might take an extra minute to create a duplicable master that has two forms side-by-side. Do this by photocopying the form you just adapted, discard the blank half of each page, and place the forms side-by-side on the copier glass.
4. Reduce the size as needed and duplicate the master form as needed for the number of students you have.
5. Distribute the forms.

If you prefer to use a customizable electronic version of the form, go to the Kjos Multimedia Center at www.kjos.com. All of the forms are available online in .pdf format for you to be able to create a more polished copy. These forms cannot be saved online, however, so plan to print out a master to save for future reference.

Duplication Restrictions

The duplicable resources in this book are strictly limited to the pages that include the following copyright notice:

© 2009 Kjos Music Press. This page authorized for duplication.

Unauthorized duplication of any other pages in this book is prohibited. The author and publisher thank you for your strict adherence to copyright laws, and encourage you to teach your students to do the same.

Name ______________________________

Write the counting below each line.

1. ______________________________

2. ______________________________

Write the counting below each line and draw the bar lines.

1. ______________________________

2. ______________________________

Form 2.1: Writing the Counting

© 2009 **Kjos Music Press.** This page authorized for duplication.

Name ____

Rewrite each rhythm line by replacing one note in each measure with a rest. Then, practice your new lines so you can perform them either by clapping, playing on one note, or improvising a melody using one to three notes.

1.

2.

3.

Form 2.2: Substituting Rests

© 2009 Kjos Music Press. This page authorized for duplication.

Name ____

Use   to complete the unfinished measures. End each line with a sense of finality. Then, practice your new lines so you can perform them either by clapping, playing on one note, or improvising a melody using one to three notes.

1. ____

2. ____

3. ____

4. ____

Form 2.3: Finishing the Measures

© 2009 **Kjos Music Press.** This page authorized for duplication.

Name ____

Three Rhythm Lines from Four Different Measures

- Write the counting for each line.
- Practice all lines by clapping, playing on one note, and/or improvising a melody using one to three notes.
- Your understanding of the rhythms will be assessed on _______________. The director will select one of the three lines and you will have the choice to clap it or play it on your instrument. Your score is based on accuracy and not by whether you clap or play.

1. ____

2. ____

3. ____

Form 2.4: Performing Rhythms

© 2009 Kjos Music Press. This page authorized for duplication.

Name ____

1. Your task is to assemble a rhythm line that is interesting—with both repetition and contrast—and has a sense of finality. Here is the first half of the line:

____

Circle the option below you think best completes the line.

A. ____

B. ____

C. ____

2. Give two reasons why you think your choice is the best one to complete the line.

   1) ____

   ____

   2) ____

   ____

3. Trade papers. Name of Reviewer ______________________

Do you agree that the chosen option is the best one to complete the line? Why or why not?

____

____

____

Form 2.5: Evaluating a Rhythm Line

© 2009 Kjos Music Press. This page authorized for duplication.

Name ______________________________

Create a variation of the theme.

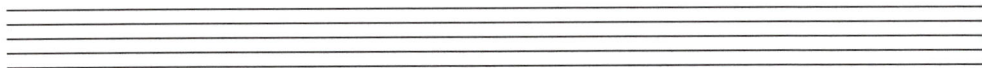

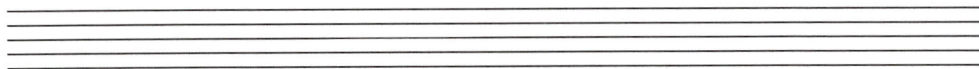

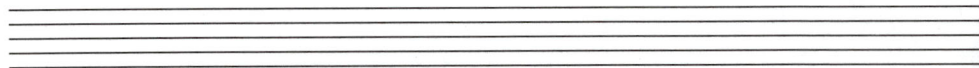

- Use the same pitches, but change the rhythm of at least one beat in each measure to
- Determine the tempo of your variation.
- Write in dynamics and any other expressive markings and articulations/bowings to add interest.
- Practice the theme and your variation so you can perform both.

Theme:

Variation:

Form 2.6: Composing a Variation

© 2009 Kjos Music Press. This page authorized for duplication.

Musical Terms and Symbols Reference Center

The musical terms and symbols reference forms on pages 50-54 are authorized for duplication and may be used to help students gather and organize information about the terms and symbols in their concert repertoire.

- **Form 3.1: Musical Terms and Symbols Reference Guide** is a quick reference every student can have in their music folder. Use the blank lines to add more terms and symbols found in the repertoire.
- **Form 3.2: Musical Terms with Illustration** is most appropriate for beginning students for whom many of the terms are new.
- **Form 3.3: Musical Terms** is most appropriate for beginning-intermediate students when they are associating terms with specific places in their music.
- **Form 3.4: Musical Terms by Piece** is most appropriate for intermediate- advanced students to use as they analyze terms and symbols used in each piece. Students may complete the inventory independently, with a partner, or as a class activity.

To prepare the forms for your band or orchestra:

1. Photocopy the form.
2. Write in some of the musical terms or symbols, as needed.
3. To conserve the use of paper you might take an extra minute to create a duplicable master that has two forms side-by-side. Do this by photocopying the form you just adapted, discard the blank half of each page, and place the forms side-by-side on the copier glass.
4. Reduce the size as needed and duplicate the forms—3.1, 3.2, and 3.3 (one for each student), and 3.4 (one per piece for each student).
5. Distribute the forms.

If you prefer to use a customizable electronic version of the form, go to the Kjos Multimedia Center at www.kjos.com. All of the forms are available online in .pdf format for you to be able to create a more polished copy. These forms cannot be saved online, however, so plan to print out a master to save for future reference.

Duplication Restrictions

The duplicable resources in this book are strictly limited to the pages that include the following copyright notice:

© **2009 Kjos Music Press.** This page authorized for duplication.

Name ______________________________

Musical Terms and Symbols

Dynamics – loudness or softness of music

pp	***pianissimo*** – very soft
p	***piano*** – soft
mp	***mezzo piano*** – medium soft
mf	***mezzo forte*** – medium loud
f	***forte*** – loud
ff	***fortissimo*** – very loud
fp	***forte-piano*** – loud, then immediately soft
(crescendo symbol)	***crescendo*** – gradually louder
(decrescendo symbol)	***decrescendo*** – gradually softer
dim.	***diminuendo*** – gradually softer

Tempo – speed of the music

	Largo – very slow
	Lento – slow
	Adagio – slow
	Andante – moderately slow
	Moderato – medium speed
	Allegro – quick and lively tempo
	Presto – very fast
(fermata symbol)	**fermata** – hold note or rest longer than its usual value
rit.	***ritardando*** – gradually slower
rall.	***rallentando*** – gradually slower
accel.	***accelerando*** – gradually faster
	A tempo – return to the previous speed

____

____

____

Form 3.1: Musical Terms and Symbols Reference Guide

© **2009 Kjos Music Press.** This page authorized for duplication.

Musical Terms and Symbols, cont.

Articulation/Bowing – the way to start or end a note

	legato – play as smoothly as possible
—	***tenuto*** – sustain for full value
·	staccato – short and detached
>	accent – with emphasis
Λ	***marcato*** – very accented
sf	***sforzando*** – accented

____

____

Style – the manner in which music is performed

Cantabile – in a singing style

Con brio – with fire; with vigor

Dolce – sweetly

Grazioso – gracefully

Maestoso – majestically

Pesante – heavy, with weight

____

____

Extra Directions – how to carry out a dynamic, tempo, articulation/bowing, or style

simile – continue in a similar manner

poco a poco – little by little

più mosso – more motion

meno mosso – less motion

____

____

Form 3.1, cont.: Musical Terms and Symbols Reference Guide

© **2009 Kjos Music Press.** This page authorized for duplication.

Name ____

Concert date and time ____________________________________

I need to recognize and understand these musical terms to be able to perform the music accurately.

Musical Term and Symbol	Definition	Illustration

Form 3.2: Musical Terms with Illustration

© 2009 Kjos Music Press. This page authorized for duplication.

Name ____

Concert date and time ______________________________

I need to recognize and understand these musical terms to be able to perform the music accurately.

Musical Term and Symbol	Definition	Example in the Music
		Title: Measure:
		Title: Measure:
		Title: Measure:
		Title: Measure:
		Title: Measure:
		Title: Measure:
		Title: Measure:
		Title: Measure:

Form 3.3: Musical Terms

© 2009 Kjos Music Press. This page authorized for duplication.

Name ______________________________

Piece ______________________________

Musical Terms and Symbols Inventory

1. Write dynamics used in this piece in order from softest to loudest.

_______ _______ _______ _______ _______ _______

2. Give one example in the piece where the dynamics change gradually. Be able to describe what happens and how to play it to your neighbor.

Measure number: ____________

3. Give one example in the piece where the dynamics change suddenly. Be able to describe what happens and how to play it to your neighbor.

Measure number: ____________

4. What is the tempo at the beginning of the piece?

Musical term: ______________________________

Meaning: ______________________________

5. Does the piece end at the same tempo it began? ____________

Explain any changes in tempo that occur: ____________

6. List the articulation/bowing styles used in this piece. Be able to explain each style and how to play it to your neighbor.

______________ ______________

______________ ______________

Form 3.4: Musical Terms by Piece

© **2009 Kjos Music Press.** This page authorized for duplication.

Endnotes

1 Wisconsin Music Educators Association, *Comprehensive Musicianship through Performance*, http://www.wmea.com/CMP/ (accessed June 1, 2009).

2 *Iowa Comprehensive Musicianship Project*, http://iowacmp.org/ (accessed June 1, 2009).

3 John F. Kennedy Center for the Performing Arts, "National Standards for Arts Education," ARTSEDGE, http://artsedge.kennedy-center.org/teach/standards/standards.cfm (accessed June 1, 2009).

4 Wendell Hanna, "The New Bloom's Taxonomy: Implications for Music Education," *Arts Education Policy Review* 108, no. 4 (March/April 2007): 7–16.

5 D. Fisher, N. Frey, and D. Williams, "Seven Literacy Strategies that Work," *Educational Leadership* 60, no. 3 (November 2002): 70–73.

Bibliography

Clark, Donald R. "Bloom's Taxonomy of Learning Domains." *Performance, Learning, Leadership, & Knowledge Site*. http://www.nwlink.com/~Donclark/hrd/bloom.html. (accessed May 28, 2009).

Corrosion Doctors. "Bloom's Taxonomy." *Corrosion science and engineering information hub*. http://www.corrosion-doctors.org/Training/Bloom.htm (accessed May 28, 2009).

Cruz, Emily. "From Bloom's *revised taxonomy*." In *Encyclopedia of Educational Technology*, edited by Bob Hoffman. Department of Educational Technology, San Diego State University, 2003. http://coe.sdsu.edu/eet/Articles/bloomrev/start.htm (accessed May 28, 2009).

Eisner, Elliot. "Benjamin Bloom." *Prospects: the quarterly review of comparative education* XXX, no. 3 (September 2000). http://www.ibe.unesco.org/publications/ThinkersPdf/bloome.pdf.

Forehand, Mary. "Bloom's Taxonomy." *Emerging Perspectives on Learning, Teaching, and Technology*. Edited by Michael Orey. Department of Educational Psychology and Instructional Technology, University of Georgia. http://projects.coe.uga.edu/epltt/index.php?title=Bloom's_Taxonomy (accessed June 5, 2009).

Hanna, Wendell. "The New Bloom's Taxonomy: Implications for Music Education." *Arts Education Policy Review* 108, no. 4 (March/April 2007): 7-16.

Marzano, Robert J., Pickering, Debra J., and Pollock, Jane E. *Classroom Instruction That Works: Research-Based Strategies for Increasing Student Achievement*. Alexandria: Association for Supervision and Curriculum Development, 2001.

University of Victoria — Counselling Services. "Bloom's Taxonomy." *Learning Skills Programs*. http://www.coun.uvic.ca/learning/exams/blooms-taxonomy.html (accessed May 28, 2009).

Zimmerman, Susan, and Hutchins, Chryse. *7 Keys to Comprehension: How to Help Your Kids Read It and Get It!* New York: Three Rivers Press, 2003.